Comparing Body Coverings

Rebecca Rissman

Heinemann Library
Chicago, Illinois

www.heinemannraintree.com
Visit our website to find out more information about Heinemann-Raintree books.

To order:

☎ Phone 888-454-2279

💻 Visit www.heinemannraintree.com to browse our catalog and order online.

©2009 Heinemann Library
an imprint of Capstone Global Library, LLC
Chicago, Illinois

Edited by Rebecca Rissman, Siân Smith, and Charlotte Guillain
Designed by Kimberly Miracle and Joanna Malivoire
Picture research by Tracy Cummins
Originated by Capstone Global Library
Printed in the United States of America in
North Mankato, MN. 082014 008463RP

Library of Congress Cataloging-in-Publication Data
Rissman, Rebecca.
  Comparing body coverings / Rebecca Rissman.
    p. cm.
  Includes bibliographical references and index.
  ISBN 978-1-4329-3261-9 (hc)
  ISBN 978-1-4329-3262-6 (pb)
  1. Body covering (Anatomy)--Juvenile literature. I. Title.
  QL941.R52 2008
  591.47--dc22
                              2008055315

Acknowledgments

The author and publishers are grateful to the following for permission to reproduce copyright material: Getty Images pp.**5** (© Raymond Gehman), **11 left** (© Lonely Planet Images/ Ariadne Van Zandbergen), **11 right** (© Visuals Unlimited/Brandon Cole), **16 middle** (© The Image Bank/Tobias Bernhard), **16 left** (© Discovery Channel Images/Jeff Foott), **17 left** (© J. Sneesby/B. Wilkins), **19** (© Digital Vision/Rene Frederick); Istockphoto p.**15 left** (© Yufeng Zhou); Photolibrary pp.**6** (© Oxford Scientific/John Netherton), **7 left** (© Cusp/Winfried Wisniewski), **7 right** (© Oxford Scientific/David M. Dennis), **10** (© Oxford Scientific/ Gerard Soury), **13 right** (© Photographer's Choice/Georgette Douwma), **18** (© moodboard RF), **20** (© F1 Online); Shutterstock pp.**4 left** (© Nicola Gavin), **4 right** (© John Bell), **8** (© Ewan Chesser), **9 left** (© Victor Soares), **9 right** (© Howard Sandler), **12** (© Mari Anuhea), **13 left** (© Juris Sturainis), **14** (© Eric Gevaert), **15 right** (© Victor Soares), **16 right** (© SouWest Photography), **17 right** (© Jeffrey Ong Guo Xiong), **21** (© FloridaStock).

Front cover of a photograph of a frog reproduced with permission of Photolibrary (©Corbis Royalty Free). Other front cover photographs reproduced with permission of Shutterstock: feather (©mmm), shell (©Ovidiu Iordachi), chameleon (©Eric Isselée), tiger (©Vladimir Sazonov). Back cover photographs reproduced with permission of Shutterstock: gecko (©John Bell), snail (©Mawroidis Kamila).

We would like to thank Nancy Harris and Adriana Scalise for their help in the preparation of this book.

Every effort has been made to contact copyright holders of any material reproduced in this book. Any omissions will be rectified in subsequent printings if notice is given to the publisher.

Some words are shown in bold, **like this**. They are explained in "Words to Know" on page 23.

Contents

About this series

Books in the **Body Coverings** series introduce readers to why animals have body coverings and how they can look. Use this book to encourage readers to compare and contrast the appearance and function of different body coverings.

Body Coverings

Animals can look very different. This is because animals have different body coverings.

Body coverings **protect** animals. Body coverings help keep animals safe.

What Is Skin?

skin

Skin is a body covering. Skin is a thin layer that covers an animal's body.

How is this hippopotamus's skin different from this salamander's skin? Which animal's skin looks smooth? Which animal's skin looks rough?

What Is Fur?

fur

Fur is a body covering. Fur is made of many hairs that cover an animal's body.

How is this zebra's fur different from this monkey's fur? Which animal's fur is striped? Which animal's fur is one color?

What Are Scales?

scales

Scales are body coverings. Scales are small, hard plates that cover an animal's body.

How are this snake's scales different from this fish's scales? Which scales help an animal to hide? Which scales help an animal to stand out?

What Are Shells?

shell

Shells are body coverings. Shells are hard plates that animals live inside.

How is this snail's shell different from this turtle's shell?
Which animal's shell is big? Which animal's shell is small?

What Are Feathers?

feathers

Feathers are body coverings. Many feathers are long and flat. Feathers help some birds to fly.

How are this hummingbird's feathers different from this parrot's feathers? Which bird's feathers are brown and green? Which bird's feathers are white and yellow?

How Body Coverings Help

Body coverings help animals in many ways. Body coverings help animals keep warm in cold weather. Body coverings help animals hide. Body coverings help animals stay cool in warm weather.

Body coverings help keep animals safe from **predators**.
Body coverings can even help animals get around!

Extreme Body Coverings

This is a polar bear. Why do you think its **fur** is so thick?

This is a chameleon. Why do you think its **scales** can change color?

Answers on page 22.

This is sea snail. Why do you think its **shell** is so bumpy?

This is a bald eagle. Why do you think its **feathers** are so long?

Answers on page 22.

Answers

The polar bear's **fur** is thick to help it stay warm.

The chameleon's **scales** change color to help it hide.

The sea snail's **shell** is bumpy to keep **predators** away.

The bald eagle's **feathers** are long to help it fly.

Words to Know

compare	look at two or more things to see how they are the same and how they are different
feather	type of body covering that helps some animals to fly
fur	body covering made up of lots of small hairs. Fur often feels very soft or smooth when you touch it.
predator	animal that hunts and eats other animals
protect	keep safe
scale	small, hard plate that covers an animal's body
shell	hard plate that an animal lives inside. Snails and turtles have shells.
skin	smooth, thin, waterproof body covering
waterproof	keeps out water

Index

Note to Parents and Teachers

Before reading

Discuss how animals have different body coverings (fur, feathers, shells, scales, and skin). Each body coverings helps to protect the animal and some (such as feathers) can also help the animal to move around. Explain to children that each body covering feels different. Body coverings can feel soft, hard, smooth, or rough. Hold up pictures showing different types of animals. Ask children which body covering they think each animal has and how the body covering might feel.

After reading

• Collect different types of body coverings for children to feel, such as leather, sea shells, costume feathers, imitation fur, and imitation alligator or snake skin. Encourage them to describe how each body covering feels and to name an animal with a similar body covering.

• In groups, children can make signs on paper about one type of body covering. Ask them to describe their body covering, draw pictures, and use decorative materials. Once finished, children can share the signs with the class, and explain what they learned.